TRINITY

TRINITY

Harry Smith

HORIZON PRESS / New York

Library of Congress Cataloging in Publication Data

Smith, Harry, 1936-
Trinity.
Poem.
I.   Title.
PS3569.M5372T7   811'.5'4   75-9546

ISBN   8180-1575-6

Manufactured in the United States of America

This book is dedicated to Marion, my wife,
who made it possible,
and to Alfred Fraenkl,
who made it necessary

Parts I & II Trinity appeared
as issue 21 of Ghost Dance.

Another section was published by
UT Review (University of Tampa)

CONTENTS

The writing of *Trinity* was attended by mysteries.

I began by setting Trinity Church and the World Trade Center in epic opposition. A month afterward they met in violent reality. May 8, 1970: after cadres from the construction site blitzed a peace demonstration on Wall Street, the church served as a Red Cross station. The mob besieged the sanctuary, trying to attack the wounded students. These events entered my narrative.

I was witness later that day to the "hardhat" march on City Hall and the melée at Pace College where ganged men with hammers and pipes beat solitary students, including girls, while policemen watched. A friend at my side disappeared in the crowd. I learned he had wandered the city in shock.

Thus *Trinity* is testimony although individuals are fictional.

While I was working on the second movement, "The Growth of the World Trade Center," someone unexpectedly sent me a copy of Erich Kahler's *The Tower and the Abyss*. What he had done in philosophy was, I found, excitingly parallel to what I was attempting in poetry. To this fortuitous intervention I owe several precise formulations, and inspiration. The coincidence was all-the-more strange because Kahler himself, shortly before his death, had urged me to read the book saying I would find it important to my efforts. I remember him, at our one brief chance meeting, infirm and shaking, telling me that he had much yet to accomplish and very little time remaining; yet he wished to speak of my work more than of his. We spoke just months before *Trinity* was conceived.

As work on *Trinity* advanced, I experienced a curious dissolving of ego, as if I had become a crossroads where vast forces converged. The work happened through me, I did not command the creation.

Trinity is epic, fusing prose & poetry. I think of it as a poem, but it might as accurately be called a novel that got loose.

—Smith

9

1 / <u>ORDER FOR THE BURIAL</u>

Ago feelings
déjà déjà
the flowering graves

The man became a boy -
old grave the new grave's maw
of dreams, and the recurring
of father's scattered bones
exposed in an open grave.

"Isn't the founder of the Marine Corps buried here?"
The man shrugged, turned his palms up.

Gleaming bones.

NOTICE:
Visitors are requested to
respect the privileges accorded
to them in the use of the Churchyard and to aid the Authorities
in preserving the sanctity of the
Graves.
Sitting on the Gravestones
is not permitted.

The man remembered a blossom Sunday in the pear orchard, his young fair daughter playing with petals, at the place of his childhood. On a swing, a neighbor boy, shouting high, and daughter laughing . . . He shook a bough and made it rain upon his daughter as it had rained upon his childhood, when he had lain full afternoons in fragrance. White, and the man knew sorrow in passing things and joy in life renewing. And in the passage of a breeze, falling blossoms reigned.

Bright skull. Startled. Beheld
Doom's grinning stereotype
eye sockets dark onto infinity
voids between the stars

Shook boughs.
White victory of bones.

                        A keening of azalea and the nooning bells —
O tarry thou the Lord's leisure
        he stayed and smelled the grass   new green surging
O tarry thou

                    THE AMERICAN STOCK EXCHANGE

sign.   Signs.   Green   Greening

gone.
                    For a thousand years   are but as yesterday
                                        and as a watch in the night
                        Scatterest   even as sleep
and fade away suddenly like the grass

                                        EXCHANGE

so teach us to number our days,

O Statistician

"- - - the damn graves bloomin every spring,"
the fat slut said.

When he was a boy the man went to Mount Olivert with his
mother to put flowers on his father's grave each Sunday. From
that ground, he would pull the dark green pronged vase stinking
of rotting flowers. That cold green metal. The dead mess to be
dumped; go for fresh water from the faucet by a rich man's
masoleum downhill. The small plot on the hilltop was green &
orderly (Perpetual Care). HAMILTON: a small wooden sign.
The boy thought there should be a headstone. With the father
was the boy's sister whom he had replaced, her death a year before his birth. From the hilltop, the distant spires of Manhattan
stood in perpetual mist like a citadel of destiny, seen yet un-
comprehended.

In Manhattan, the man checked his watch:
Late.

> Old white headstone
> head on white wings   Death's

stench of rotting flowers.

Church—Unusual   Something
Shouting   Men   yellow helmets   shouting in the street—
On Broadway.   Broadway & Wall Street in front of the church.
He walked toward angry men inside churchyard, and a short
burly worker hauled down a flag.   Red Cross Flag - into Broad-
way crowd - CHEERS - the grinning flagtaker.
   "Why did they want the flag?" Feeling stupid, John Hamil-
ton asked a workman.
   "That's a Commie flag."
   "I thought it was a Red Cross flag."
   "Not an *ordinary* Red Cross flag. There's something funny
about it."

"Who?"

"The kids in the church."

Kids in the church?

"Peaceniks," volunteered a middle-aged dumpling (Hamilton improvisded and thought this peculiar) a professional bystander. "They had this Peace Rally on Wall Street, see. The hard hats broke them up. You shoulda seen them run. Some ran in here. Some got caught, really got what was comin." A dark blue suit, a pudgy pallor. Hamilton saw. Big men armed with pipes, studded boards, monkey wrenches, hammers: hardhats.

"Those beat-on students got carried in there."

Sanctuary - the mob - Blood on flagstones

"Some students. All they study is all this Protest."

Cheering mob - workman lowering the flag of the Church THE HANOI FLAG, burned it.

Policeman

policemen smiling apologetic requesting gesturing mob back; mob growled, gave way.

A priest closed the high black wrought iron gates.

Muttering men - a shout in the crowd

My son is dead because of them.

My son is dead   My son

through muttering mobs of citymen

again

thou turnest men to destruction

thou & thousands   thou amid the thousands

and the thousands raised by thousand powers

onto the numbers of pure logic, meaningless as atoms,

snows and the powers of the suns

White uniforms white movements of ministrations
and the black of priests and the black business of priests
  In: glimpsed in an opening closing.
carved panels. heavy oak.
Young people Hamilton thought children wounded.
Blood on the flagstones
           Salami smell —
a thick slab of Jewish salami, Noticing Hamilton's stare, the
old man said he didn't know what the world's coming to, the
young have no respect, the elders lack conviction, authority is
weakening, the Chinese are waiting, yes, the Reds make student
riots and the spoiled young punks pee on the flag that gave them
everything, he never had anything and things came hard.

Hamilton walked away.

           Dogwoods, delicately
smooth and sexual . . .
O God

 God of the dogwoods
    in sex & complex white

 God in the greening
    in generations as the grass

O God of generations
     again

destruction
 Godgleaming skulls.

    wounded children
    flower children

men   destruction

ministrations & white pain

again the children
      NEITHER SHALL THEY LEARN WAR ANYMORE
construction men

Children's crusade - Wall Street $_____Broad, Hamilton placed
- The New York Stock Exchange - Steps of the Federal Building -
Children, and charging ranks
      steel helmets - yellow -
        hurt children

Fear
      watch & smile
    Policemen watched & smiled

RAISE THE FLAG   LET'S GO

LET'S GO TO CITY HALL 'N RAISE THE FLAG

URRRRRRRRRRRRRRRRRRRRRRRRRR

Lowered flags - Kent State - Hamilton Cambodia Vietnam
KENT STATE STUDENTS SHOT DOWN BY NATIONAL
GUARD - a lowering of flags - Official mourning - Schools close -
HARDHATS ATTACK PEACE MARCHERS - **New York,**
May 8— Rampaging construction workers from the massive
World Trade Center site

                                        twin monsterings skyward

a man saw - Massive complex for dense-hive, honeycombed
with costlier commerce, and the construction men marching
to City Hall, singing, GOD BLESS AMERICA

                                            masses hiving skyward
and sky like a soiled sheet.

Old magnolias, flowering -
a man's mind hurt
                        Hurt children -
and magnolias, flowering -
                        construction & destruction

children atoms snows & the power of the suns   17

2 / **THE GROWTH OF THE WORLD TRADE CENTER**

To whom the cunning suck of commerce comes,
I sing, steel members   of humanity, the growing mass
whose rising bulk portends dominion of the cube:
this athletic technocracy and its perfection of rigidity,
of works & systems & their sources, structure & utilization,
of programs & computations, units & uniformity, con-
    formity & the continuous process and continuous frame, con-
    ventions of columns & beams, continuous walls skyward
Hamilton outgabe.

Alas, poor Hamilton, a skull. He held his own death. He gazed at
the death held in his hands, and it was small & absurd, and
Hamilton was small unto himself
and gone

JOHN A. HAMILTON
1924-
Son of Nancy Arlens & Thomas Hamilton
Member of the Association of the Bar
of the City of New York, partner in
the distinguished firm of his father.
Devoted husband & father, he did his
Best for himself, his family & his
Fellow Man

19

And Hamilton wondered on goodness & the good and the good in his life, vaguely in weariness like a weight of the infinite unknown forces onto & beyond him, a mononucleosis of history in him, this sickness into a vertigo of commerce & abyss, and he knew a dull confused despair he had not known before

O God which art the idea of the Good
and all ideas of good

O God which art the holy greening
and the sacred white of love

O God which art the dream of Perfection
and the perfection of dreams

O God which art the theory of the rigid frame
we kill the greening & the love

"God is that which none greater can be conceived."

But, listen: I say Satan is inseparable: god & the devil
are one in the perfect weld, the divine daemonics
of the rigid bent,   this unspeakable skywardness
Hamilton outgabe.

Commerce & Abyss

Derricks in the sky

The man stood before the tower of world trade grown tallest and beheld the cloud-high derricks as tyrannosauri on some stern height. Man's own tyrannosauri - We put them there.

Behemoths in the sky

How did we do it?
a man thought:
How did we Get up there?
How did we Get to here?
How Come?

Onward & Upward

honeycombs of commerce

Hive

the buZZy borogrove of business
Bigly

Gimbels

cubic tower of World Trade

entrepreneurs, bankers, brokers, investors, architects, engineers, construction men, exporters & importrers & all the captains & crews of World Trade

Swarming

workers

   "*Like bees*," Hamilton heard the old farmer, his summer neighbor in Maine.

   "I was readin in a magazine about somethun - some kind o rockets I guess - you could just strap to your back an go anywhere you like, needing no plane, just that little thing like the astronauts have. I seen the astronauts usin one o them - little flying machine."

   "Suppose all the people going to work in New York City could fly like that," Hamilton mused. "They'd be bumping into each other and everything."

   "That'd be a sight I wouldn't care to see," Jappy said. "I dunno they'd be like bees, Bejesus, like a swarm o bees!"

21

Form follows function,
En masse   utter it   *En Masse*
Technology's Democracy of the relentless interchangeable
Equality, the collective and the collective of the collective
workers swarming to their functions
                         Kingdom come
                              the Kingdom of the Cube

                         Entfremdung

technics tactics techniques   technology $\leftarrow$ – – $\rightarrow$ teleology

techniques   – – – $\rightarrow$ ethics

–values–   standards   norms   routines

Mobilized, for efficient action formed under the rules of Science,
the Modern Man I sing

dung dung Entfremdung

     Hamilton telephoned his office: "Unavoidably detained."
What would they say? -
If they knew what he was doing. Thinking.
And Margaret wife, what would she   ? She might understand,
with cool disdain.   Aloof, lovely, pale lady of great halls.

Her breasts . . .
At Salzburg for Don Giovanni in the Felsenreitschule
her decollete as she leaned to him her breasts   the full mystery
of white like quick blossoms, translucent to the blue delicate
complexity of veins -
and dark nipples glimpsed.   the long necklace of pearls
with the emerald carbuncle between her breasts.
Flesh, ornament, a loveliness of mad elegance
A fair contract.   No,
        he would not
tell her.

No one.

No one

Crowd, in transit on Church Street, lunch hour pedestrians, traf-
fic of motor vehicles, the Hudson Tubes, himself, the human flux
                he saw the seething
                Center
    of World Trade, rocketpack flitestrians entering & ex-
    iting, multitudinous tiny portals on all floors, humanity
    swarming about its hive towers, buzzing busily, here and
    there

Absurd.   He felt despair, childlike utter helplessness. near tears.
        He lit a Balkan Sobranie cigarette, and sighed in, painful-
ly. Crowd - human beings - numbers - swarming
No One

Margaret.

                    No
he gave her   Predictability, Access & Success
                     the town house Bar Harbor the World
;She   Predictability & Cultivated Pleasures
                     the art of elegance   emerald on flesh

          Decay
               . . . . the manhole to the underworld at his feet
                     sulphurous gases steaming
he knew
                    the infinite void under the glittering surfaces &
                        exquisite structures, the brilliant design
                        of his life all his works and advocacies:
                            individual rights while individuals
                            are invalidated, penal reform while
                            humanity goes to hive, Margaret?
Why did he love her?

The Truth.   No need for Truthsaying.
Perhaps she knew.
                         Ennui   Abyss

Art of emeralds and breasts.
A fair contract.

     Hamilton went West on Liberty Street.

[the old Engineering Building   No crowd

                              DURABLA
                 twin sculpted symbols
                              the globe girdled by starstudded steel

                    DURA   BLA

no
                                        north side Liberty razed O
            bliterated   *O*pen   Site. World Trade
                             a girder UP
NO
crowd /
    I can see you're a man who don't like crowds.
voice. elevator man young black. / Subway. / St. George in
Brooklyn. Man Hamilton had entered empty car, shunned one
still loading in people. Operator spoke, surprise, closed doors im-
mediately   UP
    "I don't like them either," he told Hamilton.
    "It must drive your crazy, all those people packing into here
all the time."
    "It does."

UP   derrick
                                                    tendrilled
                                                    cables

                        the ascension of a girder

                guy ropes
                 the riggers

                Ascension   some new birth
            fro Bethlehem steel   what birth
            of   steel   the birth of Non
                                            Life   beyond life

DURABLA

            Business is our most important progress.
ABstracts.
abstracted from life   :   ONGO
abstract life   Non Life growing
            Systems are our most important products
abstractions things tools government industries institutions
organizations works of worldnon

                Non accreting
                    by units

NON

life beyond life

by units dynamic accreting

god

the girder

Hamilton
the man crossed Liberty to stand
under the girder

with the riggers:

a man

```
= = = = = = = = = = = = = = = = = = = = = = = = = =
----------------------------------------------------------------
= = = = = = = = = = = = = = = = = = = = = = = =
```

Under the girder the man (small spasm at his lower spine) watched the casual riggers guiding, as passersby glanced danger-
thrilled overhead, hurried on. He stayed, in stolid awe
= = =the riggers & their easy motions, the girder midway, sway-
ing, ascent momently stopped.
Godlike   works   <--------> a foreman's wave   uP
godlike   sweatblotched blue denim shirts profane
     a wave   sinister
       as a secret muscularity.

              God in the girder   O
              God the rigid frame

                   this building
             Prince of this world
             Our will be done
             God & Satan one

Hamilton in
The Moving Target mystery novel by Ross Macdonald who read
Kierkegaard read the gulf looked into is innocence lost here at
some edge he looked his life & lives
down , a building up outgabe /

But what innocence was I?
The man had a conviction of non-innocence not guilty of the
world. Perhaps he looked down some other gulf. He did not
know.

He beheld a raucously reverberating generator
named JOY, and from the tower emerged a
low great jetliner as if spawned by it.

building building

building our doom, Margaret   *our children*
                                                          in herit

              construction
casually
              causeways conduits condominiums computers
              our children
smiling doombuilders

beehive tombs

beemen

behave behive

BEEMAN

Be Man

our units to the stars

What is all this?
man thought
what is all this
to the stars

31

3 / **DAY OF THE EARTH**

Once upon Hudson's shores beached whales
Heaved & shook, shook earth and the gathered men,
Through their feet the life throes in the land,
Resounding and receding like the waves
of the lessening tide. The fathers of the church
with whale spades, axes and long knives
Cut-in, Great God, the yet living flesh,
Flensing in long spiral peels fat thick blubber
which the women tried out in coppers
on the beach. Oil, soap, and from the head,
spermacetti candles; steaks hewn from the small.
Thus the leviathan nourished the church.
Governor Ben Fletcher therefore chartered
Trinity for salvage of wrecked whales
from the High Seas.   Where that rough strand had been,
a man walks straight concrete athwart steel frames
for which New York pushed   Hudson's piered banks
westward far, and no whales roil this thick marine.

And on the erstwhile strand, the man
resonated to a raucous red-named generator JOY
,,,*(joy machines*
,,,*erection ecstatico*
     Automation
men construction men

and Captain Hamilton, Korea, saw a blown man unbleeding
thrashingasp like a bleached whale

all Weifts Wrecks Drift Whales

                                thrice off Amagansett
                                        the blow

of whales in his childhood, only   tiny geysers near horizon

and not again

     1696-Hamilton
and whales perhaps close to common as the porpoise packs sport-
ing in the Sound his summers at Rocky Point when foxes ran
along the shore by his grandmother's place *the funny red dogs
from the woods, Grandma* woods which went along farther than
eyes eastward around dunes into dark blue distances of blur
cliffs. Perhaps as Manhattan had been in the fullness of the
whales

     a fair land to fall in with ,

Henry Hudson.

                              River North
                              River From Beyond
The Mountains
Ka   *Ka Ho*

te da

Kahoteda

                        acetelyne
          man's lightning   man's lightning dream

                              new higher towers without spires

and in the guiding gyre Noght
                    Noght was
Noght was foryeten by th' infortune of Marte
                    Episcopal whales and Grandma's woods
the carter over-ridden by his carte

PEDESTRIAN TRAFFIC PROHIBITED

John Tower for 608.   one man - one job.

Markets are becoming segmented, Hy Steirman said.
The granddaughter of the arc welder is mad.

Automation and the man, I sing,
Under the wheel

The man recalled the gone forests of youth, the fine-tailed foxes
from the oak, chestnuts, the grandmother cliffs beachplummed
and the supplanting cottages, the flux of people outward along
the long shore, inexorable.   Too much.   Too much built
upon the world of his childhood.   Levittown was the potato
flats of central Long Island.   The Wantagh woods encom-
passed by the Phipps and Browning estates had become other
Developments.   The thought of Openness.   Filled lakes
and buried streams.   *Landfill,* he stood on landfill.

The gones of youth. The forests of the past.   Inertia
        inertia of species   inertia of science
     inertial guidance of humanity, unmanned,
         automatic. the ongoing institutions systems onto
                                          systems

Let bygones by bygones?

                    No more chestnuts

                    The Future

of man and earth
Under the wheel
full lowe
i sing

                                        EAT SHIT   Eat shit
the steam of a pile driver pounding saying
Eat   shit Eat shit,
as on Earth Day

        dandelions and cigaret stumps in the park
City Hall sooted gray, Hamilton's Earth Day
                        Dear Lord the Sky
a vision through a yellow filter, sunny morning
April, First Annual Earth Day 1970:

    The man's bowels were loose. Denying impulse, he tightened
his buttocks, strode resolutely toward 14th Street (Healthy Ex-
ercise). The steam engine stopped. It occured to him that the pile
driver's words might have been influenced by the state of his shit.
He wished his mother had never encouraged him to eat Grape
Nuts .   He determined to give it up Once & For

the pile driver started anew with a different beat   ALL   ALL

        Steam engines, Fathers
        Fathers of all this ALL
                        that's ALL
        Father of this All

cars courts Pucci neckties secretaries smartly
                bargains business bar air badassed bitches

UNBELIEVABLE

you better believe it!

Chinese women softly

      Hamilton's progress indifferent to the streets,
seeing a great spider weaving in a vanished clearing.

                              Beggarman Bowery
liquor store pawn vomit snore   Strawberry
farm; biking back after picking
Sun sweat clean dirt   garbage streets

under the wheel

                                      breasts
bouncing BRA*less* gently   breast
flesh form
      etched
tight against the white fabric
         / cotton T-shirt

                      transparency

deep rose through a white screen

                 sweet loll

blue jean girl flower child
                  a calm smile,
she looked at him, and he blushed. He smiled to her hurriedly
(like a Fool, he thought) and looked away. He wanted to talk to
her to reach to touch /
he hurried past.

flesh, flesh, all this flesh

Ashamed.   Only a few years older than Carol.
Unashamed.   Early woman, flowering
Carol would be
ashamed.   Private school.   The Graces.   What would she
be?
become? what   what would the world be for her?

stereothink   future

SPEED

Carol, good girl, believed in Ecology. Riding on a pony.
Bicycles. Jet/ / travel
MOD
Population Control
          Love   Margaret,
What could we
what world

The world is passing away

and all its lusts
and all its things

        things   speed sex

speed   pills

     narcosis & barbed sleep

Sleep

                      God the greening and the love
                flesh   earth   day
                            crowd

       rubbing   crowdrub

       crowd   ALL   crowdALLcrowdlust
                    lusts   *frusts*

DIS

                                       ant

from dung   ENT

THE NEW YORK TIMES

      swirling

Our shit, I sing,
under
the girder and the wheel
all earth and life I sing

LIB
id in us

LIB
      servo
women

           chanting circle

WOMEN'S LIB

marching

                sweatshirt
                  she
                sloven

                        Decidedly unattractive
                        Hamilton decided

GET

YOUR

PIECE

FLOWERS

hippy hawker   O, peace

EARTHDAY PEACE BLOSSOMS
          bosoms
peace   blossoms   japanese
                                                          white

orange
          white

               orange & white
                         blossom   beautiful
               against the vast

                                             of sky

                    the silence

                    the cold serene

                                   no sensation of falling

          parachute
                    very
          small   **43**

hanging in the sky

terrain
rolling hills a forest a lake roads buildings   what   looked like
a village
pretty country   typical American scene
*   like parts of Virginia*

It was spring in Russia

Francis Gary Powers

landed.   *a plowed field a tractor and two men*

MAYDAY 1960.

It was spring on 14th Street and John A. Hamilton EARTH-
DAY   and the mild stagnant sky of the city, dull-shimmering
and *AN EVENT UNPRECEDENTED IN THE HISTORY
OF* loudspeak *THE WORLD* Union Square green Spring in
Russia and Hamilton had seen Spring in Russia on 14th Street
Francis Gary Powers U-2 descending into Russia "Like parts of
Virginia," Gary Powers said, and a long-legged girl was walking
the looker with his hand in pocket found himself scratching his
balls   *Ballscratcherno.* Hamilton snorted. Our doves the dirty
pigeons flapped over heads of politicians in the park.

children

yellow moonflower

redletterday

Green Earth

green & white

childsplay.
      concrete   children & chalk

                                   children   green

            (children & flags
                green & white

) like US Flag

            But

               green & white
            what did they call those flags?
The man would ask his daughter   SAVE
                                       child
                                     Our   sign
                                     TREES

Our Trees
                  ghastly elm
         Hamilton hated
the elm in his townhouse garden.   *blue blue glowing ghastly elm*
the damn floodlights, Margaret.   It eeried his nights.   Like a
scene from another planet, Purgatory or the Far Future, *that's*
right. Of course it was all right in the day and popular with guests
at night.

"I loathe it."

*"Our light show, Darling? I think it's like some marvelous
electric sculpture in fiberglass."*

"It makes the tree Something Unnatural."

"You're so silly sometimes, Darling, but I love you "Margaret, arching, Cat.   Sensuous & arch, Margaret of white.
Artifice & flesh.   She made herself into a work of art.   Pari-
sian styles, a body proud /

poise, grace and breasts   *a gell*

electric elm

Margaret's beauty

the man saw old oaks after ice storm.
Icy oaks in the sun.

OUR FORESTS

THE OCEAN IS DYING

reproduction of diatoms

Photosynthesis

Union Square, greening

Spring

la la forsythia
and the flowering girls
loving all in greeno

The man thought he thought of sex more in periods of stress
STRESS-----SEX---

In times of stress, sex
stress sex   intense stress--------desperate sex

Hamilton felt as though he had made an important discovery.

In the street of messages, amidst the bazaar booths of air pollution water pollution radiation war Socialist Workers sewage the
placards of every exigency CANCER / AIR he lit a lavish cigar-
ette THE POPULATION TIME BOMB *all this sex* deep-called
the smoke like a captive spirit in his lungs. ZERO POPULATION
GROWTH /
orgies random Roman
promiscuity Sodom & Gomorrah
S & G   homo
sexuality Mass sadism porn
ographic *Entfremdung*   *mass sad isms*
Hamilton punned it.   MASS TRANSIT
        Dravidian Gonds

                                        Into the Future

            and young dancers, swaying
            to the west

            NOISE POLLUTION
            decibels   physiological harm

                    transistor

                    radioheads

            A stereotype girl, with false
            eyelashes fluttering, Smiles & gave

he glanced,

and threw it away

a little girl. Thin beautiful, perhaps nine.
long darkblonde hair in a breeze

If only it were that simple, Hamilton wished

technological solution to technology?

                    :POLLUTION POLLUTION onewordrock
                        & roll, liturgical,
                electric music
                instruments amplified
                            lified
                            electric sex /
that beat like an artificial heart /
                            freehaired dancers
Stop. & Go
                            like traffic
wearing hideous masks.

                The Noise
hurt Hamilton's head. He deemed it Aggression,
The chanting dancers seemed in a trance.

Rock, Stop. Shake °° the fine-formed young dancers moved
mindlessly NOW Like zealots Now like zombies Life / Death -
zeal zomb - Cry Life dancing Living Dead - the heart mechanics-
NON . NOW - Hamilton was puzzled.

Thoomp Thoomp the pulse in this man's temples, aching, beat-
ing heart : : : : : *hurt brain* bombardment : : : : : : : : : : : : : : : : : : :
circumstantial matter sensory, like nature amplified   AB

                                        incomprehensile
                        Blare

decibel despair.

Score hope percentiles.

Hardhat Day, Earthday and all designated
days
Doomsdays

                        liberated breasts
                            the dead beach, re-
                            inforced concrete
                                        Ship's shore

No more thinking about Earthday *what good does it do you, John, you think too much* his mother told him. Today would be called, yes, Hardhat Day, when the men hurt children.   Yet what was it that he had witnessed? What was it really? More than half the world away how many children lived or died in horror today?   Why was that less real?   It was less real here. It was 2 p.m. Wasting Time.   Hamilton, guilty, would return to work and work late.   But why guilt?   Were his thoughts less important than his work?   Ideas of life & non-life, or briefs in admiralty law?   Sometimes he thought his work was separate from his life, and that must be some kind of sickness, he thought, - the common sickness?   Still that shipowners' law could command him, overrule Deliberations he knew to be more important, and he would soon go back to his law. First a cup of coffee.

Petie Agnew's. A cup of coffee in the steamy Greek's. Hamilton felt he could not eat. Behind the counter old Petie was excited, talking "------------------The Ninth Wonder of the World. "When I am little shaver we have outhouses and woodhouses and we go swimming in the buff off South Ferry, lots o' oysters, so I tell you this going up has got to be the Ninth Wonder. Hey! Listen to Jack Hammer."

listening looked outward to the work and out

Old Petie had seen Changes. Hamilton saw a boy's odyssey from Aegean isle to massed Manhattan *Petie Boy. enough of changes*

Carol   the future now

un.
units / building to life STANDARD AUTOMATION SYSTEMS
un / un

Caught in canny dread: FUT   RIGID   REG
SYS SYS SYS
Was that the *future*?   *Is?*   The future *was*.
The werewish.

        nowdreams green go
            flying hope, of farther futures wished --
within & without our power.

In Maine, late spring at Northeast Harbor, the cottage of the lilacs in the night that night, of conception. Yes, God, conception.

Hamilton felt sure he knew. That night - the simple wildness - must have been

>> Ago.

fucks, work, fame future.

daughterwoman. Hamilton felt listless.

a spent shad.

>> The shad were journeying
>> up the river to the Hudson Highlands,
>> more shad than people
>> in the city, to spawn
>> in waves the generations of the shad
>> and the generations of man and the great May
>> run of the lilac

>> *shad rack*
>> *Me shad?*
> *shad roe* - How did it go? Hamilton
>> didn't know much

about popular music.

"Shadrach, Teshach, Abednego," Old Petie answered.

Hamilton realized that he had spoken or sung aloud. Embarrassing.

He put a dollar on the counter and left, feeling Awkward.

Across the street, Southeast, another razed
corner, Greenwich & Liberty, littered; three young clerks played
catch with a football; crabgrass was coming-in-strong before the
dig, ailanthus jungling along a back boundary. The tree of Hea-
ven flourished always, in ash & rubble of inner city, its blighted
places and untended yards abandoned to that lush redemption.
Hamilton found curious poignancy in the life of the vacant lot.
He thought of wild raspberries, how they grow, best prospering
in the shelter of decaying homesteads and collapsed barns and
sheds and out of rusty derelict vehicles in overgrown pasture and
along fallen fences and by the sills and up through the Maine
island where raspberries burgeoned from the ruins of rude shacks
which once were fishing camps. Raspberries in old ruins.

Learn ethics from the shad.

The shad running, heavy with roe, successions,
and the soon, lilac culmination, the run of
the lilac shad.
                    Of Shad and men, I sing,
and all the particles of life
                    and of Hamilton who also
saw himself a particle of the successions
                    and, unspeaking, cried
Damn you, I am infinite.

Yea, the infinity of man and the power
                of life beyond man
                the wonder of water
                carbon & its compounds
                of sun and genes, of DNA
                determining and the
                indeterminate particles,
of that which always is
I sing, at the end & beginning of mysteries.

The indeterminate particle determined.
                name: Speck
          did murder in the techno
                name
archetype
          mass murder mass man known as Speck.

The werewish is upon us.

      a sickness in life Hamilton life itself was sick

      Martin Eden

                into the ocean

Once upon Hudson's shores, the namegiver
sucked-in a wind of flowers off the Jersey meadows.
He paused, that blunt captain, unmoving,
unknowing of his calm smile. The pleasure
of that landsmell! Pollen, resin, leafy earth.
So sweet one Dutchman did not know What
had greeted them. A mariner, wading,
with cutlass did-in a seven-foot sturgeon
for a common feast. The richest of rivers!
Such sturgeon and the shad and striped bass surged
in the fertile meeting place, the river's
slow sea-mingling; mackerel, silver hake & bluefish,
menhaden for fertilizer, cod and herring
and anchovies upstream at the strong freshening
joined carp and sunfish and yellow perch in a long wide bay.
More, an estaury full of oysters,
blue crabs teeming in the shallows. Finding,
at that landfall, fame of mink and otter,
muskrat and beaver in hardwood highwilds
with many wolves and deer, easy heath hens
and huge wary cats, and such gabble of turkeys
hunters shot only for twenty-pound-plump,
O Providence, all said For Ever.

Hamilton, in his city, dreamed
                         the land's last fragrance.
Running a gauntlet of gorp, shad still swam
in hordes upriver into the future.
A man willed them into the future.
He commanded the elements.

> Of the numbers of shad and men,
> Of law and banking and the suns,
> I sing wild raspberries and world trade.